He Is ... Therefore, I Am

S H A R A N Y A   D I N E S H

AuthorHouse™ UK
1663 Liberty Drive
Bloomington, IN 47403 USA
www.authorhouse.co.uk
Phone: 0800.197.4150

Published by AuthorHouse 02/15/2019

ISBN: 978-1-7283-8432-0 (sc)
978-1-7283-8431-3 (e)

authorHOUSE®

He Is ... Therefore, I Am

Foreword:

Babuji Maharaj has given a detailed description of how an abhyasi should be:

One who is:

"Soft-spoken, straight forward, loving, duty conscious, good at heart, always active, humble, polite, willing to transform himself, intent on doing his daily sadhana, always willing to serve the Master and the Mission, willing to surrender to Him, one who respects others, one who lets ego, one who recognizes his faults and rectifies them, one who is not stubborn, if at all, stubborn to cut off his desires, stubborn to achieve his spiritual goal, one who always cooperates with the Master."

The journey from I AM to HE IS, is the journey of every seeker, the journey of becoming an abhyasi as Babuji describes above. Some may start from the beginning, and many may join with some distance already covered in their previous births. But, this is the only true journey worth undertaking. Sharanya has traversed this path and claimed very humbly at every juncture or turning point that her journey has "just begun"! With such humility she tells her personal spiritual journey while all along explaining the Method, and the Mission too, in a very subtle way. She tells us about the sublimation of her ego – in the most unassuming way possible!! So, those who read this book and also know how to read between the lines will know what Sahaj Marg is all about. Sharanya writes so simply and straight from the heart that it touches the heart, brings tears and the longing for Him.

I would advise everyone to read; all those who already are on a Spiritual path – to vicariously participate in the experiences of a co – traveller and even those who are yet to begin; so that they feel the urge to "catch up".

Wishing her His Blessings on this journey,

Shalini Nair

14ᵗʰ April 2017.

Mentors ...

In this beautiful journey, many have helped me blossom. I met my master (spiritual guide) only once but I have received His love incessantly from many quarters. All my learnings have come from my Guru, delivered through different people, His instruments. Thus, many people have touched the life of this seeker and I have learnt invaluable lessons from all of them. I owe too many people to be able to individually acknowledge all of them. I attribute it all to my Guru and His way of teaching me to be sensitive and discerning. My mentors are many, thus the learnings are also innumerable. I wish to especially thank and express my deepest gratitude to some and seek pardon from those who I have inadvertently missed.

Foremost, I am indebted to Shalini. She was instrumental in my becoming an *abhyasi*. Had she not been a family friend, I would probably still be in the dark, searching and tearing myself apart. Thank you, Shalini, for being a part of my friend circle. You brought me to His doorstep. The first year you gently pointed out the mistakes I was continuing to make. You never rebuked my continuing follies, but steered me in the right direction and opened the right doors for me. You encouraged the spirit of faithful *abhyaas* and learning through experience. Thank you once again.

Secondly, thanks to my prefect, Sister Chanderkanta Arora. She gave me my first three sittings. Her nature is such a contrast to mine; and these very differences helped me grow and challenge myself to the limits. In trying to understand her zest for Mission work and madness for master, I fell in love with master and tried to become integral to the Mission. Her drive and untiring ability to work pushed me also into doing things which I never thought I was capable of. The spirit of volunteering came from her. She encouraged me to write and express myself, so this book is also thanks to her. Thank you, aunty.

In sister Chanderkanta's absence, when she was stationed in Chennai and then shifted to Kharagpur, all of us were taken care of by Late. K.N. Rai uncle. He devotedly travelled every week from Chhattarpur to Indirapuram and gave us sittings (a two-hour metro train journey). His utter simplicity took my breath away. He always shared innumerable stories and narrated excerpts from master's books, explaining the finer points and small technicalities of this Method. Simplicity, absolute surrender and how to serve without the feeling of servitude were a few things he taught me. He did everything out of love for master and tried to instil the same feeling in us. He is not amongst us anymore, but his memories are always with me and continue to guide me.

Another couple I wish to mention here are Sehra uncle and Promila aunty. I am very grateful to master for bringing Arun Sehra uncle and Promila aunty into my life. Consistent self-enquiry and persistent efforts to improve myself is what they taught me. Sahaj Marg is ingrained in every aspect of our lives; this is what they showed me. I cannot just follow this path, I had to learn to become one with it; I needed to live Sahaj Marg, and I learnt this from them. Learning never ends and knowing only Sahaj Marg is not our master's aim; that would merely make us frogs in a well. Master encouraged the study of scriptures and wanted every abhyasi to read and learn about other philosophies; I understood this after meeting them. They showered love on all of us and boosted our kindred spirit. We became family and true brethren because of them. Thank you both, dearest uncle and aunty.

Last but not the least, I wish to thank our Scribe, the person who is instrumental in giving us the wonderful messages from Babuji (our second guru); our whispers from the Brighter World. Without having the good fortune to meet Babuji, she has brought His messages to me and made me feel very close to Him. Babuji's countenance is the first face I saw during my third sitting. This scribe brings me closer to Him with every message she receives and sends us. This scribe is apparently very unwell, and lives in confined quarters; she has not stepped out of her home in a long time and it is her unblemished love for Babuji that enables her to continue to receive these messages. I will never be able to meet her either and yet I feel very connected to her. She has indirectly answered many of my questions and I am truly indebted to her. Every single message means the world to me and has helped me in more ways than I can elucidate.

Thank you.

Preface

I started Sahaj Marg at my lowest point in life. I was in a state where I did not know where anything was headed and what exactly was my purpose in life, if there was purpose at all, was also doubtful. I still cannot definitively proclaim that I know where this life is headed, and my search to give purpose to this life continues. Yet, the one thing I can emphatically state is; the biggest difference that has happened to me is, myself. I am no longer who I was before this journey commenced and every day that passes by is a humble reminder of His presence in my life. His guidance in enabling me to shape this life the way He wills it. That is the purpose, the goal of my life. He is my Guru, God, friend, mother, father and enemy too, at times. I cannot fathom a moment or a thought in which His presence is missing or an event where I fail to see Him or sense His presence by my side. He is everyone and everything to me.

Thank you, my beloved Master.

This journal is my humble attempt at describing His presence in this nobody's life and how He has given meaning and purpose to this wayward wanderer. There is no possible way in which I can express my gratitude; this life is His and every breath I take will fall short if I have to return the debt - the grace and favours He has bestowed on me.

I humbly attempt to start this beautiful journey with a special message from 'Whispers from the Brighter World'. Due to copyright issues I am unable to put the whole message here, as I would have love to. Luckily for me, all is not lost. The link is permissible and here it is: http://www.sahajmarg.org/babuji-maharaj. The date is Monday, November 2nd, 2015: 10:00 a.m.

All the mistakes are mine and praise is His, the ugliness is mine and the beauty is His. It is because He is … therefore I am.

Contents

Joining Sahaj Marg

This seeker's life tells a story of a life replete with change and learning since 2008. My life took a definite turn in February 2008, and I ceased to be the same person ever since. Every day I unravel something new, and the feeling of awe increases. Ever so gently over the past decade, He taught me acceptance, patience, and surrender. He fuelled the desire for self-enquiry and self-analysis so that with diligent practice, the divine goal of this life will become achievable in this lifetime itself.

If an astrologer were to draw my birth chart and make predictions, he or she assuredly would have put down 2008 as the epiphany year of my life. Most of my life prior to 11 February 2008 seems like a hazy blur. Mindless passing of days, years, and overcoming the challenges or rejoicing in the good moments without really being able to be aware of or experience them. By the end of 2007, it became a deluge of challenges, and all my efforts to assuage my stormy mind became in vain. When He gives, He simply does—totally unabated and unleashing everything in one go. I was being pushed into abysmal pits without a sliver of hope, accosted by hurdles created by my own convoluted thinking. I was barely hanging on to my sanity. This was my plight when I joined Sahaj Marg.

I needed peace and calm. I was desperate for a path which could channel my turbulent state of mind, a sliver of light in the darkness that kept bombarding me day after day.

Prayer, meditation (on my own), philosophy (reading a shloka from Gita or reading our scriptures) have been integral to me. Fasting, performing all the ritualistic pujas, reciting "Hanuman Chalisa," and visiting temples were second to my nature. All these activities took a feverish pace when my mind was at unrest. None of them seemed to help me or give me the answers though. To sprinkle salt over my wounds, even after ever so doggedly leading the correct life and praying for change or peace, nothing seemed to change, and peace was still very far from my grasp.

Things happen when they have to happen, and nothing is a coincidence. Everything—even the falling of a leaf—is predestined and happens at the appropriate moment. This is how Sahaj Marg happened to me.

On 11 February 2008, unable to put up with anything anymore, I showed up at a friend's office. I knew she was into meditation and asked her to guide me too. She steered me in the right direction and gave me an address of the prefect (trainer) who would help me get started. Without further ado, I called the number and sought an appointment.

This prefect was in the same apartment complex, and my sittings started the same day. Something that I was searching for from the age of sixteen finally crystallized. He made me wait so long; or rather, I took so many years to make myself heard by Him! "When would He listen to this story of mine? And that too direct from me?" *Complete Works of Ramchandra, Lalaji*, p. 129). My wail was, "When will He listen to me, make this nobody's heart His abode?"

The moment I stepped into my prefect's house, the first thing that greeted me was a series of photos. All the walls of her apartment were covered with photos of our three masters—Lalaji, Babuji, and Parthsarthiji. She had a separate huge one of Parthsarthiji and another one of Babuji with an enigmatic smile, dewy eyes looking straight into heart of the seer. She had two huge bookshelves brimming over with books. Being an avid reader, that was an exciting discovery for me. I was too wired and nervously excited to pay attention to anything else. Just those eyes, looking straight into my heart, made a deep impression.

My prefect is a dynamic person with a very disarming and effusive smile and a dominating personality. She gate-crashed into my morbid existence and extracted all she could and helped me blossom and fathom the full potential of this method and the wonders diligent abhyaas can do.

After my first sitting, I felt euphoric. If flying were a challenge unachievable, I would have excelled in it. I felt extraordinarily light, unburdened, and free. I felt as if the weight of the world was lifted off my shoulders. My smile, which had disappeared over the last few months, was back again. The wait for the second sitting seemed too long, and my expectations knew no bounds. I prepared myself to 'really fly,' set myself free, and soar high after the second sitting. But contrary to my expectations, my second sitting turned out to be very emotional and anticlimactic. I could barely hold my tears, and thoughts played a tyrant that day. Every thought descended—disarrayed past, mixed childhood, grievances. Everything flashed in front of me, and I barely experienced anything. I remember being disappointed and crestfallen that I had failed or fared very badly. A subdued me returned home that day. My feeling of lightness continued, and that was a grace. I fervently said my prayers to God (I still could not associate with guru or master), seeking His help in allowing what was best for me.

I went for my third sitting with a blank mind. No expectations apart for a simple prayer that I get some direction in life and know the meaning or purpose of this life. My third sitting was beyond explanation. I have never been able to give exact words to what happened during those thirty minutes. One moment I was flooded in light, and then suddenly, it was totally dark. Then I saw a figure clad in pristine white with an ever so gentle gaze, loving, dewy-eyed. That beautiful person extended His hand and lifted me off my seat. I held His hand, and He guided me through a flight of stairs and a dark passageway. Then suddenly, there was only light and nothing beyond. I tried to see beyond the light, shielding my eyes and searching for this person, when I heard, "That's all." I was snapped out of a beautiful reverie and realized I was wet-eyed. My heart was exploding with inexplicable emotions. I searched my prefect's eyes for the image I just envisioned. It could all be my imagination and hyperhallucination too. I was too dazed. I kept shaking my head, trying to get a grip over myself, when my eyes fell on the picture on the wall. This was the same face—wet-eyed, gentle, loving face, looking into me and smiling. I asked my prefect who this person was and she said, "Babuji Maharaj, our second guru." So I was not hallucinating after all, and that was a big relief.

My first three sittings were signals to me that my journey had finally begun, He had come to assure me that my wails and pleas were heard, and henceforth, I would have direction, a purpose in my life.

Abhyasi Beginner

The first three sittings and my very enthusiastic prefect gave me the right environment to be a disciplined and dedicated abhyasi without wasting a day. I can proudly claim that I started my abhyaas the right way, the method as prescribed, from day one. Being a voracious reader with a general lifestyle that confined most of my time within the four walls of my house provided me with the ideal opportunity to read the mission literature from the very beginning of my practice.

I will never be able to repay my debt to my prefect. She has been ever so encouraging and dedicated. I am not sure if every prefect is expected to take such good care of the newcomers or if it was unique to her. Or perhaps it was my master's doing that I was blessed with my sittings from such a committed prefect. Whatever the reasons, fortune continued to smile on me, and I was embraced by this prefect very lovingly. She truly nurtured me in every way. Her dedication to this path kept me on my toes. I was stupefied at her devotion and the time she gave to the mission unflinchingly. Even at the oddest hours of the day or night, her doors were ever open. In case I missed a sitting, she would call to check if I was faring well and demand the reason for my absence. She magnanimously opened her library to me, and I was able to read some very old publications of the mission. She knew my strengths and weaknesses and filled in the gaps herself. She forced me to participate in volunteer work and invited me to accompany them to the ashram.

Her dedication both amazed and irritated me. My understanding of the mission, master, and the method was too limited, and her magnanimity overwhelmed me. She appeared crazy, whimsical, too forceful, and kind of intoxicated all the time. And there I was, a stark contrast to her, mild, ever so cautious, and laid back. I give all credit to her and her forceful ways that I could come out of my comfort zone and really learn and be involved in this wonderful mission from my early days. Most new abhyasis hesitate and want to practice their way, at their pace, and probably mature after five to ten years of such snail-paced abhyaas. Thanks to my prefect, who took this decision out of my hands, and however frustrating it was for me at that time, her forcefulness worked in my favour. In my own earnestness to excel as an abhyasi, I practiced diligently, volunteered and tried to participate in all the activities she summoned me to, even if it was ever so grudgingly on many occasions. But it all worked to my benefit, and in no time, Sahaj Marg coursed through my veins.

And it is all thanks to my prefect. My abhyas raised many questions and reading the mission literature gave me my answers. At my prefect's behest and after reading *Spiritual Yatra* by Toni Bernardi, I was seized with a strong craving, a fervent longing to meet my Master, the one person who had been working on me for all these years and finally placed His benevolent hand on this pauper's head.

This paragraph from the book was the clincher- *"India 1979: I remember that Clara, who was sitting just near the door of Lalaji's room, had exclaimed, "Ale'! Now He is walking away!"*

He did not see the persons. He only felt what was emanating from them, and perhaps he had said aloud what was only a thought. I do not know. This is only an idea. But Babuji's words always had a meaning that went beyond the words themselves.

In this moment, as I am writing, I have understood the real meaning of his words. What he wanted to say to everyone there, what he really meant, was that he loved each one of us in the same way as each one of us loved him. Those words did not refer to me personally. It wasn't that he loved more one or the other. In fact, he had not said, "I love Toni," but, "Toni loves me," which is different. It was only my love and my devotion for him that attracted "as such" his love. Babuji was like a mirror. He only reflected what was in front of him." (Spiritual Yatra, by Toni Bernadi)

I was mesmerized by these lines. What kind of love was this? Do such people live anymore? Can one person love everyone so abundantly, unrestrainedly, be totally giving without any expectation of reciprocation? I had to stand in front of such an embodiment of love, feel His eyes on me and be washed by that wave of love. I was propelled and magnetized into going to Chennai, to meet this 'embodiment of love'.

After a long debate with my better half which involved him weighing all the pros and cons of such unplanned trips that primarily included unscheduled expenses, the inconvenience of not being at home when required, coupled with disrupting the children's schedule by making a trip in the middle of a school session which was undoubtedly detrimental to them. He also commented that such behaviour was reckless and uncharacteristic of a person who was meditating; the whimsical nature of this spontaneous and irrational decision. I still managed to hold my ground and get my tickets to Chennai, with the children in tow.

Despite so many negatives, I put my most stubborn front and remained unyielding in my request. This is highly uncharacteristic of me because I hate confrontations or arguments. Usually, I abruptly make one statement, my two bits, and then I clam. But, this time try as he might, my partner knew, I could not be swayed, he yielded and willingly planned my trip; I had made up my mind. If he opposed to send us I would have probably asked for a loan from a friend or family member and booked train tickets. That was the kind of frenzy and urgency that hit me. So, on 28th March 2008 I entered Manapakkam Ashram, Chennai, our world headquarters.

Seeing Master

Apart for seeing my Master, many other thoughts were playing havoc in my head. Introspection brings a sense of shame and I acknowledge that I entered Chennai ashram with many fancy ideas and very little true longing to meet the embodiment of love. My stupidity and inherent egoistic nature was very gently brought to light by Master in many different ways during this visit and many times more in the years to follow. This was just the tip of the iceberg. Over the years, many more flaws of my persona have been brought to light through meditation and His grace. Every day, I look at the mirror in this ongoing journey to earnestly see what He wills me to be, and not see what I wish to see. 'Mirror mirror on the wall, let Him reflect in me, that's all'.

My prefect had continuously appreciated my progress and I foolishly concluded that as being 'the sought after ideal Abhyasi' for Master. Secondly, everyone said that Master sought out the new abhyasis and met them in person. They did not have to wait in long queues or stand by the gate waiting to catch a glimpse along with the crowd thronging to have His *'Darshan'*. My trip to Chennai was laced with such egotistic thoughts; I was the best disciple, Master would be waiting to meet me. I am a new *Abhyasi,* so again, I need not wait in queues. In fact, with my performance accolades He would invite me inside, so I was assured of much more than His blessings!

Anyway, armed with these dreams and fantasies I entered the abode of my Master (He was still a mystery man to me then).

With utmost efficiency and alacrity, I settled the children in the family dormitory area. I gave them the canteen coupons, arsenal for their hunger pangs and left them to their resources.

My feet barely touching the ground, I glided through the ashram premises and very soon presented myself at the Master's cottage main gate where I saw a huge crowd, already waiting. From the looks of it, the way they were settled down with portable chairs and mats spread out, some seemed to be sitting there for hours. Now, how was I to go in breaking the line and go barging inside the gate? This was a big dilemma. Secondly, when did I become so important that I rush ahead of all these already waiting *abhyasis*? I crept close to the gate where an abhyasi brother was monitoring the crowd and calling out names of *abhyasis* who could pass through the gate and enter His abode. I stood there for a while, simply soaking in the ambience, the surreal architectural beauty of the cottage, its serenity, the peace and beauty of the whole place. I tried to envisage Him inside, sitting amidst many aspirants and discussing important matters, or maybe sharing a joke with His dear ones. Chennai ashram, and every ashram, as I have experienced in all the ashrams I have visited so far, has a unique environment. The minute I stepped inside the ashram gates it was like being transported into a different world. A sublime, light air prevails here. Every face looks relaxed, at ease and smiling. Everyone is carefree, with an air of gay abundance, inner laughter and serenity. I later discovered that many abhyasis were waiting for more than 5 hours, yet no one had a sense of urgency, irritation or restlessness. He weaved His magic without stepping out of His sanctum sanctorum. He seemed to transmit patience and surrender and cover the abhyasis with a blanket of acceptance. They were waiting, in a prayerful state, calm, stoic and brimming with faith.

Three hours went by and I saw no sign of anyone allowing me inside the cottage, nor were there any signs of Master coming out, I started to get a bit fidgety. Day one was fast coming to a close. I had planned only a two-and-a-half-day trip. I had imagined a quick, instant meeting today, followed by proper leisurely introductions tomorrow and hopefully some chit-chat the following day! Here, day 1 was slipping through my fingers with not so much as a scent of Him; forget seeing, introductions or talking to Him.

The people waiting by the gate saw my morose face and asked me to send in a note, mentioning the fact that I am a new *Abhyasi* and wish to meet Master. I complied, without any waste of time, and sent in the note.

Someone said, "Call the secretary, and say that you wish to meet Master, you are a new *Abhyasi*". I acceded to this suggestion too without a demur.

Someone else said, "Speak to Master's right-hand person, if he can call you inside he will do so in a second, because he is always by Master's side. Make a request to the brother who is in charge of organizing the master's schedule!"

Believe it or not, I did not leave this stone unturned either! I called my prefect, asked for that brother's number and placed a call requesting permission to meet Master! Everyone heard my pleas, said they would do their best and at their earliest, I should remain calm and patiently wait by the gate to be summoned inside.

What has to happen, happens and all these gimmicks are but gimmicks. 'We plan and He laughs' is a very true phrase. He has to take mercy and turn His gaze upon us, then alone can anything happen. Till then, wait and pray. That is all I could do and that is all I ended up doing the next day, too.

Master did not come out for His usual evening talk with abhyasis, nor did He make a short trip on His golf cart to the medical centre. I was not called inside, and He did not step out. In fact, by 6:00 in the evening, the gate keeper brother announced that Master would like to retire for the day. He is tired and requests all abhyasis to vacate the premises and return home. He bids us 'good night' and will see us in the morning. That announcement pretty much sealed my fate for the day and I very despondently dragged my feet back to the dormitory. One day was gone. My confidence took a beating and I began to wonder if I went wrong somewhere. Why did He not come out rushing and embrace me in His arms? Was I not a 'worthy Abhyasi'? How were Toni Bernardi and I different? Plagued by such thoughts, I slept fitfully and a very contemplative and subdued I presented herself in front of the cottage on the 29th morning at 6:30 am. With renewed hope and a fervent prayer in my heart, a smile on my lips, I stood in front of the Master's cottage. The gate keeper *Abhyasi* brother was there, he recognized me and said, "So early sister! Please attend Satsangh (group meditation), have breakfast and come. Master will come out today, or you will be called inside. I still have your note."

I did not want to leave my spot but acquiesced and left for satsangh, attended to the children (I asked my cousin to come and collect them, so I could be unfettered) and was back in my spot, in front of the cottage gate, by 10:00 am. The wait had begun. Morning drew to a close and I was patiently waiting, for a glimpse of my Guru; nothing happened.

Master had many meetings lined up and was busy, and by lunch time, we were again asked to leave because He would like to rest a while. When we were asked to return by 3:00pm I was downcast and near tears; my second day was also half gone. Now, I was totally lost. Why did He not call me in? Why did He not come out either? Would I be able to see Him at all? Forget talking or introducing myself. All that fancy nonsense was gone, I was now desperate for a mere glimpse. I wanted to be able to see, that is all. Even from a distance was alright. My return ticket was for tomorrow and today was fast slipping through my fingers. I could not eat anything. My throat was dry and I was feeling heavy, laden with disappointment. My floodgates would have burst open with a single sympathetic word, or touch at that moment.

I was up to the brim with such intense unknown emotions. Was this love for Him? I do not think so. How could I love someone I was yet to meet? Then why was I so sad, teary and desolate? Why was I continuously praying, ever so fervently? I had come with such grandiose thoughts and here I was, reduced to a pathetic beggarly state of mind. A mere glimpse was all I was compromising for now. With these thoughts, I walked up to the bookstore, absent-mindedly picked up some books and wandered about the ashram, waiting for the clock to strike 3:00 pm. There is a mango grove behind Master's cottage. Inadvertently, my absent-minded wanderings lead me there and I sat under that tree and cried my heart out. Some unknown grief, a nameless pain in the heart, and I could not control my sobs nor hold back my tears anymore. I sat there, just me and my miserable self, and cried. This became my favourite spot in the ashram for all my future visits. I sit under this tree and soak it all up, the calm inside in stark contrast to the chaos outside, the stillness amidst the bustle. It works like a balm for my frayed nerves and helps me gain strength, to introspect, recognize and overcome my weakness.

I was back at the cottage gate at sharp 3:00 pm and resumed my wait. By now the gate keeper brother had come to recognize me and said, "Sister, you will surely be able to go in now, or Master is likely to come and sit on the porch, so you will be called inside. Please wait."

I gave a broad smile (must have been my first smile in the last 2days) and felt recharged. Finally, my never-ending wait seemed to be coming to a close. I thanked the brother with a smile and started looking expectantly at the main door of the cottage, hoping to catch the first glimpse. Very soon though, as the dusk set in, it started to dawn on me that I was to be dejected today too. No news from inside came and none of us waiting outside were called in either. People waiting outside the ashram gates started to talk amongst themselves, one *abhyasi* said, "This is the first time that Master has stayed in for a stretch of 48hours. This has never happened before. He usually comes out at least once every day and meets us."

Someone said, "Most evenings He either sits on the porch regaling us with anecdotes of His experiences with His master, or walks with all of us on the ashram premises, imparting His wisdom laced with humour and wit."

Listening to all that talk my self-esteem took a dive and hit abysmal pits, I was certain it was my presence which was causing Master to stay inside. He was aware of my overrated thinking of myself and He was ever so silently showing me the mirror. I felt dejected, bereaved and very alone the evening of 29th, as I walked back towards the dormitory, still a failure; 'Master would like to retire early. All the abhyasis please leave the cottage gate. Come back tomorrow morning after satsangh. Good night'

I could not sleep a wink that night. I was leaving tomorrow evening, what if Master stays in yet again, another day and I board the flight back home without setting my eyes on Him? Should I ask my husband to extend my tickets for a few more days? My husband may probably say 'yes', he knew how keen I was to meet Master, and would have been sympathetic too. But the bigger fear was, if I did risk my husband's ire and extend my stay, Master may still decide to stay in and I may still end up waiting to catch a glimpse of Him. What should I do? I tossed and turned the whole night. My children asked me if Master had called me inside, if I met Him, even my husband was calling and asking if I got my special Darshan! It was a bizarre, unreal and un- savoury experience for me. Ever so gently came the dawn of 30th and I must have dozed off with these thoughts, sobbing into my pillow.

Yet again, I mustered courage, made a fervent prayer, "Master, I will just see you from afar. That is all. Grant me this wish, please" and again took my post by the cottage gate at 9:00 am. The gate keeper brother said, "Sister, you are having to wait too long, hopefully Master will come and sit on the porch now."

I dared not smile or feel encouraged this time. I gave a careful, imperceptible nod and continued my wait. Master did not come and sit outside. But mercifully the gates opened and His golf cart was parked near the cottage door! Master was getting ready to go to the medical centre. Finally, He was at least coming out. I will be able to see Him.

As I had promised to myself, I did not crowd near the gate nor did I plan on running behind His cart, and neither was I going to push the crowd and pounce on Him. This time, I would 'see' Him from afar, and become worthy enough for Him to summon me in His presence.

With all this happening at the cottage gate, concurrently I placed a call to my cousin. We would have to leave for the airport and the kids were still at her place. Thus, when it came to the most crucial moment, I found myself half waiting near the cottage gates so that I could get a clear view of Master when He came out and the other half I was a sentry at the main gate, waiting for the kids. As fate would have it, both the big events happened concurrently.

I was halfway between the cottage and the main gate when a throng of abhyasis ran towards the cottage gate because Master had stepped out, and exactly then my cousin called saying she had reached the main gate with the kids. I did my fastest sprint that day, yanked the children from my cousin and sprinted towards the medical centre with the children racing behind me, wondering about my sanity.

Huffing and puffing I managed to reach just in the nick of time and luck finally smiled; Master passed by my side smiling radiantly and tapping the children on the head with His walking stick, blessing them. My joy knew no bounds. Both the children got a pat on the head and were blessed. My long wait had finally fructified. I had seen Him, my Guru; it was from a distance, it was for a mere few fleeting seconds, yet

I was exultant. The feeling is indescribable, when my friend asked what I felt, I spontaneously replied, "I am in love." I am not sure how that answer came. Did I love Him really? Maybe it was more an overwhelming feeling of gratitude than love. How could one fall in love with a mere fleeting glance? Was it possible? I have no answers to such queries; the reply came straight from the heart and my love for Him grows every second from that day. And I did not 'fall' in love, rather He made me 'rise' in love. And it keeps rising unabated and ever ceaseless.

Coincidences

That fleeting glimpse of my Master was my share during my first visit to Chennai Ashram. The pompous Sharanya that had gone to Chennai with a grandiose air was left in Chennai, for good.

A subdued, introspective and grounded Sharanya boarded the flight back home. This was the first change I saw in myself. With a mere glance, He held a mirror and helped me see and really know myself for the first time.

I was not sure when I would be able to meet master next; or when I would be able to visit Chennai again. I wanted to be worthy of Him, that became the purpose of my life. This was possible only through diligent *abhyas* and bringing about a positive change in me. My fickle mind finally had one focal point, a goal to this vagabond's, aimless life.

But what we grow up with, the baggage we carry and the belief system which is so ingrained in us supersedes and creeps back, very determinedly and menacingly. The layers take a long time to truly depart and my first year was spent waging this very war. Much to my misery and as a dare probably, many coincidences came to light between Sahaj Marg and my life. To narrate a few:

I loathed missing Sunday Satsangh; and thus, most of our weekend travels came to a grinding halt. At times my husband used to put his foot down and drag us to some holiday resort or to a weekend getaway. One such trip was to Naukuchiatal, a quaint hill station, in the state of Himachal Pradesh, India. I had missed the preceding Sunday because of some pressing duties that I do not recollect now. So, I was very much looking forward to attending the coming Sunday when out of the blue we headed off towards the hills. I was crestfallen and managed to make my husband feel very guilty too.

My husband had booked us in a wonderful resort and my family was trying to cheer me up. In the room, they opened the windows on all sides and excitedly showed me the Himalayan peaks, a lake on the other side and lo behold! my husband spotted a board which read 'Sahaj Marg meditation centre'. At first, I thought he was pulling my leg. But in that wilderness, in the oddest and vaguest of destinations He had setup an ashram. It *was* our meditation centre. My joy knew no bounds. I attended satsangh, took individual sitting and could see the Master's cottage, next door. It was the best trip I had; a spiritual holiday. This was no less than a miracle for me. Another such coincidence:

One Wednesday Satsangh, my prefect showed us a thick, hard bound, brown coloured book. She passed it over to all us abhyasis and allowed us to take a peek; she emphasized that we handle the book with utmost reverence and care. She said that this was the first volume of Whispers, messages from the Brighter World. This book is like the Bhagvad Gita or more for the seekers on this path. When my turn to take a peek came, my riddled mind conjured this burning question. "How was I faring, so far?" I opened the book seeking the answer to this question. Call it fate or Master throwing the rope so long in front of me that I could get further entangled, the page that opened was my birthday date. And Babuji addresses it to the scribe, as His daughter.

For the same reason (copyright issues), I am unable to put the whole message in print here. But like before, here is the link, http://www.sahajmarg.org/babuji-maharaj ; and the date this time is: Saturday, October 25, 2001- 10:00 am

I did not read the whole message, just the beginning 'My daughter' was enough for me. It re-affirmed that this path was for me, that I could progress, and get my answers on this path. How could it be possible that from a book with 1000 odd pages, spanning almost 3 years and so many dates, I picked this one date that was singularly meant for me? This definitely was a message and one which was meant exclusively for me.

The common thread in all the Mission books I have read and continue to read is that all of them focus on 'love' …

Transcending from human love to universal love and moving on to divine love, culminating in becoming love. My third sitting ended on 13th February. And I had begun this journey as an abhyasi on the 'Day of love' 14th February. Today, I can't believe that my thinking or my train of thought used to be so ludicrous and my mind drew such ridiculous conclusions too. But this was how my mind worked, to put it succinctly, I doubt if I had a mind at all.

This is just the tip of the iceberg. Very soon I found out that Babuji and my daughter share the same birthday. This set my heart singing, not only was I special, my daughter was even more special! My stupidities did not end here and as I write, I sadly acknowledge that my so called erudite self was truly very ignorant.

To add insult to injury and seal my ignorance, I got to know that Master's grandson's name is Bhargav and our daughter's name is Bhargavi! I never thought there would be so many similarities and all this was too much for me to ignore without giving them some special meaning or attaching significance to them.

The icing on the cake is my identity card number: INSMAE 786. Now this definitely must have some meaning was my thought. Of all the numbers why did I get the most unique, auspicious number? What was He trying to tell me? I don't know. All I know now is that despite all these good omens and so-called special signs Master made me wait for three long years before I could meet Him face to face.

Omens & Signs

Not only were coincidences a whim I practiced and paid heed to, I subconsciously catered to many superstitions, had dogmatic thinking, was adapting very rudimentary method of worship, attached exceedingly great significance to omens and signs and habitually thought through every event with utmost gravity and seriousness. All these qualities were my excess baggage and I was continuously paying penalty for indulging in them, following them, and yet failing to relieve myself of these needless excesses. I brought them with me when I joined this path.

I had a beautiful marble temple, adorned with idols of Gods and Goddesses, painstakingly selected and acquired over the years from all the holy places I had visited. For all important decisions, I put my question in front of my Gods and waited for some signal, a sign of approval or disapproval. Even after joining Sahaj Marg, I involuntarily continued with the same philosophy. I bought photos of the Gurus' and with utmost reverence placed them in my temple alongside my Gods. The only difference was that now I was seeking answers from the Gurus too, along with the Gods. Unfortunately, ingrained habits tend to grow with age and get further embedded, becoming our character.

Meditation brings in an awareness, discernment to know the right from wrong, it enables one to think and decide for oneself. Meditation enables us to listen to the inner voice, the tiny voice forever trying to guide, and the very voice we ignore over the worldly clamour we are perpetually lost in. Cleaning (the second step in this path) helps get rid of the grime and needless baggage, what we collect every day and what we have been hoarding for a long time, consciously or unconsciously. It brings in a state of calm amidst chaos, a balance between our material pursuits and spiritual aspirations. Night prayer (the third step of this path) is equivalent to having a tete -a - tete with Him, talking to Him about the day's proceedings, the changes I still seek and the help I need to be able to improve myself.

On the verge of completing a year in Sahaj Marg, regular practice and apparently doing everything correctly, the change in me seemed to have stopped. I still had no grip over my anger, I continued to live under a cloud of illusions and refused to let go my excess emotional baggage. My habit of holding grudges, and having unrealistic expectations continued and to sum it up, I think my meditation had become rote. I had not changed an iota, in fact, if I looked at myself closely I was worse than before. I sat in front of that temple and sought guidance from 3 extra photos now. I was like a spider; desperately trying to free itself from the web; instead the web seemed to be getting thicker and creating a worse vice like grip. What had gone wrong, or where was I going wrong? Why did peace and calm continue to elude me?

I was beginning to question the efficacy of the method. One morning, sitting in front of the temple I was churning these very thoughts when my husband remarked, "I thought your meditation was all about self-enquiry and self-awareness. Here you are, still seeking answers from these Gods." I barely heard the rest of his litany, he had made a passing remark, but it had found its mark. I had joined a new path, seeking change, and yet I was doing the same things! I was continuously opening the same window and foolishly expecting a different view. How was that possible? My husband, without joining this path seemed to have figured this fundamental truth. And, after one year of arduous stupidity I was still clueless, wondering where I had gone wrong.

I carefully dismantled the temple that day, bid adieu to the pictures and brass idols for good. That day, I gave away my most cherished possession, the marble temple along with all my Gods and guardian angels, and felt unbelievably unburdened, fearless and relieved.

That night my prayer meditation took a different turn. I sat for a long time and allowed the tears to flow. I waited till I could feel the presence of my master, knelt before Him and prayed for change. And change happened. Sahaj Marg has given me, and continues to give, many chances to better myself. One by one, Master relieved me of these baggages and helped me travel lighter, with just what I needed, ample to get me from here to my destination.

May be that is why Sahaj Marg, my life and the people in it share so many coincidental similarities. So that I get over the undue importance I used to give to them and stop making a fool of myself. Whenever my thought process went awry and every time I make such a faux pas, Master has delivered the message I needed to learn and reiterated the importance of believing in my inner voice and learning to ignore such omens, signs, coincidences and frivolous similarities.

I had embarked on this journey with three separate entities in front of me, Me: - Sharanya was one, God: the second entity – the one I was trying to realize or know and now the Guru- the connecting link between God and me. Probably that is why I had relegated the Guru to God status and put those pictures in my temple. But these instances helped me introspect and the gradual change in me augmented my faith in the system. Somewhere, without my conscious awareness, the demarcating line between God and Guru had blurred and disappeared into oblivion. Guru and God had become one, and they were together very live and playing a very interactive role in my life. I was unable to keep the God-Guru in the temple anymore; that was a distant separate spot outside of me. I wanted them inside me, in my heart. They belonged there, that was their temple and abode. With this change in my thinking came another realization that this is what He was trying to tell me all along. We are not separate, not 2 and 3 people like I had imagined. We are all one, God- Guru and me too. Thus, in trying to realize God through the Guru I was actually trying to realize myself. Myself was becoming wiser and more of my Self, under the constant tutelage of my Guru. This is the end result meditation under Sahaj Marg path offers to every true seeker, meditation for Self-Realization.

Over the years, this 'meditation for self–realization' graduated to 'meditation for Human Integration'; which is the larger and long run Goal of this wondrous path; Sahaj Marg.

Family and Environment ...

My first year as an abhyasi was a tumultuous one. The challenges were many and seemed to be increasing every day, testing me to leave the mission, or checking if I had the nerve to continue against all odds.

Primarily, going for Sunday satsangh was a challenge, the ashram was 25 kilometres away and to be able to attend satsangh I had to leave at 6:30 am. The earliest I could return was 10:00 am. In the interim the children would be up, ready and waiting for breakfast. The whole family was put to an inconvenience, and my husband would be in a bit of foul mood, having me packing off on a Sunday morning, when it was the only day he was home and could be pampered, and have a relaxing day together. Before joining the mission, Sunday used to be the most laid-back day, everything happened at a turtle's pace and after joining this path, Sunday became my busiest day. This was a bit hard to digest for my non abhyasi husband. He was forced to make the biggest sacrifice. He saw no charm in my bright and chirpy demeanour at 5:00 am on a Sunday morning. Late night outs on Saturday's became a headache for me. I insisted we keep all partying to Friday or no party at all! The friction between us was very palpable. And the worst part was, everything was immediately attributed to my joining meditation.

I changed for the worse after joining meditation. I refused to go out. I did not enjoy partying. I stopped non - vegetarian eating and cooking! I was angry that he did not see the good change I was trying to bring in myself.

Instead of being the good sensible husband, encouraging me and joining the mission so that we could both practice together, this man seemed to get annoyed and uptight whenever any mention of ashram, or meditation came up. He 'allowed' me to go and do whatever it is that I was doing for my happiness and peace of mind, that in itself was a great contribution and I should be thankful for that. Expecting him to join in and having me run away every Sunday for satsangh, leaving the family to fend for themselves, he had definitely not bargained for.

Wednesday was alright, he was at work and I could do what I wanted. All these rules and regulations and doing things around his time and in his absence, was getting to me. Grudgingly, the first year I never attended more than one Sunday satsangh. I tried to be regular for Wednesday satsangh. I never did any volunteering and even when I went for Sunday satsangh I sat by the exit door and the minute the prefect said, 'that's all', I hurriedly made my way back home. It was more of pseudo attendance and a sop to my conscience. This kind of abhyas seemed hypocritical to me and rebellious to him.

My prefect updated us about upcoming training programs, Satkhol (our Himalayan ashram) visits, retreat centre opportunities, or Master coming to Delhi and conducting a satsangh. Most of the time, I felt despair and hopelessness. The thought of quitting was always at the back of my mind, I was unable to do complete justice to the method. My duties at home were not going to change in the near future and my chances of attending *Bhandara*, or a training program were far-fetched. I should probably join after 10-15 years when I will be free of responsibilities and home duties. But I was already left with only half my life! I did not have another 10-15 years to wait and then rejoin, hence my sense of urgency was strong too. This was a far cry from the utopian state I had dreamed of achieving after joining meditation. On the contrary things were topsy-turvy like never before. I had successfully exchanged my calm unruffled existence and given a carte blanche to tsunami.

Amidst arguments, frictions and misunderstandings I continued my *abhyas* as best as I could through the first year. Despite all the gripe and disapproval, I refused to leave the method, and continued to do my *abhyas*, my husband relented marginally. It became evident to him that I would stay on, I had found my way and I would definitely continue this journey to the end. My husband is still a non *Abhyasi* and it took me a lot of self-explaining to convince myself that it was 'okay' to be a non *Abhyasi*. I wanted him to join too, by any means possible. Most *abhyasi* couples attended Sunday satsangh with the feeling of enjoying a 'spiritual picnic'. I longed for that environment at home. If he became an *Abhyasi* the journey somehow would have been smoother, or probably our relationship would have been a better one, more compatible and with a common ground; this was my expectation. Today, it makes no difference. Each of us comes with our own share of karmic baggage. Who wishes to shed it, lug it or add to it is all person dependent. Moreover, joining the Mission was not qualification for being the 'ideal' person was my learning; each to their own. In fact, I feel it is more a failure on my part that I am unable to show enough change so as to attract a single member of the family to join this miraculous path. Sadly, I still am the only *Abhyasi* in my family. I have been a miserable failure in this respect. Today, I have no grouse against my husband and his rationale to remain a non *Abhyasi*. Instead, I pray that I become what Master wants me to become and mould myself to His will.

Seeing my commitment and sincerity my husband did not have the heart to stop me or hold me back. Instead, he encouraged me to attend every Sunday satsangh. He started making breakfast on Sunday's and I returned home from ashram much calmer and free of mental clutter. Thus, one satsangh changed to 2 in a month and I soon started attending every Sunday. My home and people around me changed and accommodated to this changed lifestyle of mine. Master had worked His charm and been by my side through the year. Everything and everyone seemed to be rigged in my favour and thus came my chance to put my application for attending the upcoming *Bhandara*. So, I prepared to attend my first *Bhandara* in July 2009; from the 22nd of July to the 25th of July, being held in Tirrupur, a small town in the state of Tamil Nadu, Southern India.

'*Bhandara*, is like a gathering where one could bathe in and experience ambrosial showers 24/7' this is the description my prefect gives. The grace of the living Master and the preceding Masters could be partaken. It would be as beneficial as being able to drink a drop of the elixir of life and attain spiritual immortality. Speedy progress was doubly assured for people who attended the *Bhandara*. The disciple, who is likened to a piece of charcoal is burnt at intense heat, purified and comes out a glittering diamond from such spiritual congregations.

This was music to my ears, it seemed attending a *Bhandara* was equivalent to becoming infinitely spiritual. Or at least abhyaas getting an automated upward trajectory and reaching your goal at jet speed. It meant, changing fast, becoming worthy of Him, getting a chance to meet Him …

First Bhandara

JULY 23-25, 2009, TIRRUPUR.

On the last day, my husband got cold feet, and my daughter (then a 5year old) glued herself to me, saying she would also come to meet Master! In a flash, I saw all my plans of peaceful meditation and spending all my time meditating in HIS presence being washed away. If my daughter was coming along then I definitely would have to spend more time with her and sneak in for Satsangh. I was already simmering with resentment at this change of events but couldn't do much to make things favorable for myself. So, an angry Sharanya, saddled with a subdued 5year old daughter, boarded the flight to Coimbatore. Through the flight, I kept weighing my options on how best I could make this work. What could be salvaged of the already destroyed peace of mind and how was I to get back my state of elation at being able attend the *Bhandara*? I did not want my daughter to feel guilty, the poor girl was just 5 and could not be blamed for wanting to tag along. The whole debacle put a complete damper on my *Bhandara* euphoria.

The banner stating, 'Welcome to all Sahaj Marg *abhyasis*' greeted us when we reached the exit gate at Coimbatore airport, and this managed to lift my veil of sadness and my spirits were buoyant again. I was sure it would all work out fine. These brothers and sisters had come to receive us. We were escorted to the buses which would take us to the venue. My daughter and I were all smiles and eagerly boarded the bus. The short bus ride from Coimbatore airport to Tirrupur, the venue of the *Bhandara*, is beautiful. I cannot recall much today. All I can recall is that the scenery and calm outside helped me surrender to my situation, stop complaining and go with the flow, be gracious and imbibe some calm and beauty I was seeing. I was determined to make the most of whatever was possible. I cheered up and started showing the sights to my daughter, slowly getting her also to normalcy.

The *Bhandara* venue was bigger than anything I had ever imagined. It was like a mini township in itself. I was staggered by the sea of faces and the busy hustle bustle everywhere. The aroma of coffee filled the air near the reception area. Many abhyasis had already arrived. I could see small groups of abhyasis huddled together, laughing and sharing anecdotes, enjoying coffee. They all looked relaxed and happy. Very soon we were guided to our tent, in the comfort dorm. The huge tents and camp like environment excited my daughter too and we happily settled ourselves in our corner. We freshened up and went on our search for the children centre. We had mutually decided that during morning satsangh time, my daughter would continue to sleep till I returned. Then I would be with her the whole day. For evening satsangh she would go to the children's centre and participate in the different events they were having. Thus, I could be with her and attend my satsangh too, most beneficial arrangement. She agreed a bit reluctantly, but she had no choice anyway. I was determined anew to get that shine; even a little grime washed off would be miraculous.

So, as decided between us, on the evening of the 22nd, I took my darling girl, packed with food, books to read, toys to play, and set her up in the children centre. She was sad, a bit weepy, but held back her tears, gave me a weak smile and asked me to return the minute Master said, 'that's all'. I was more than happy to oblige (I was going to attend satsangh, and that was enough for me) and promised her that I would return at the earliest.

I chose a spot from where I could see the Children's centre and was also close to the exit gate, so I could leave early in case she cried, or someone came looking for me.

That first satsangh of my first *Bhandara* was the longest one hour and the most chaotic one. I was restless, my mind kept going back to my daughter; wondering if was she okay, if she was crying, or if she wandered out of the tent searching for me, I kept opening my eyes and checking the time, wondering why was this going on and on, maybe I missed hearing 'that's all' … and so on … It seemed to be never ending and the way I raced out of the meditation hall and rushed towards the children centre, I sealed my fate for the next 3 days.

My daughter was sitting exactly where I had left her, her eyes glued to the gate, trying to spot me. She had not spoken to anyone, nor had she eaten anything, played with her toys or read. Through the hour, she was simply sitting in that corner with her eyes fixed to the gate, waiting for me.

I knew she would not say no if I forced her, but of her own volition she would not step into the children centre again. That was a closed chapter. So, my evening Satsangh was gone. I was still maintaining my good cheer. Morning Satsangh was still in my sights. I could attend the Satsangh and be back by the time she woke up.

When things are not meant to happen, they just don't. I was fated to stay away from the meditation hall, not be able to have a glimpse of my Master this year too. This was the bigger plan He had for me, and here I was, silly me, scheming all sorts of ways and means. My daughter woke up at 4:00 am bright as a lark and smiling. The first question she asked me was, "Can't you sit here, by my side, and meditate?"

I was resigned to my fate now, today was the 23rd and the *Bhandara* officially started today, five Bhandara satsanghs were considered imperative, (my prefect said so) and I was already being forced to miss the first one.

I sat by her side and tried to meditate, but I could only cry from sheer frustration and helplessness. All the spite and venom I had felt at being stuck in this hole, and the inevitability of being unable to crawl out of it, raised its hood afresh. Most irrelevant thoughts came back with a vengeance and I was seething again. I barely managed to keep my temper in check and be civil. There was no point staying on in Tirrupur now. As far as I was concerned the *Bhandara* was over before it began. I would definitely not be able to attend satsangh, so staying in this tent was a waste of time. I might as well head back home and get on with life. Through this thought process, I was beginning to feel certain that Sahaj Marg was not for me, after a year-long wait, this was definitely not the way events were to unfold for me. Again, being unable to set eyes on the Guru, being trapped in the tent and missing every Satsangh, ambrosial shower was far away, I wasn't even worthy of a drop. Probably, this method was not for me, or nothing could polish this piece of coal, I was ordained to be thus, a piece of coal, unto death. The search had to go on, I needed to search for some other path and redeem myself. This was a waste of time and so I should head back home …

I called my husband, told him how I felt, and asked him to immediately bring our booking forward. I had no intention of staying here doing nothing but cater to my daughter. So 24th early morning flight is what I asked him to reschedule the tickets to; he should book now; and sooner the better. The *abhyasis* in the adjacent bed sensed my state. They were seeing my frustration and struggle to attend the satsangh since last evening. They over heard my conversation with my husband and the tension within me was very palpable. A lady came up and gently tried to console me, saying, in a *Bhandara* grace is everywhere. This grace or transmission is not limited to the meditation hall alone. Where ever we are, we could and we should be in His remembrance and the work on us continues to happen 24/7. A few friends I knew also came and tried to drive some sense, pacify me and persuade me to stay on.

Was I listening though? I had made up my mind and I was waiting for my husband's message confirming the changed schedule. Without a demur, and further discussion my husband acquiesced. He cancelled the existing tickets and sent me new tickets for 24th morning. I packed our bags, and spent the rest of the day with my daughter, took her to the canteen, played with her inside the tent. I would bid adieu tomorrow and probably search for a new path, I did not know. Whatever fate had in store for me; peace reigned for the rest of the day and I did my evening *Puja* in the tent, with my little girl by my side. We walked up to the main gate, booked a taxi to the airport and retired for the day, all set to board the flight out on Master's birthday.

The next morning, we were wheeling our suitcase to the taxi stand area when my mobile phone beeped. Thinking it was my husband checking my progress, I glanced at the phone to confirm it was from him. But the message was from the airline authorities and it read, "All flights scheduled today are cancelled due to unforeseen circumstances. Your ticket has been rescheduled for 25th at 3:30 pm. We regret the inconvenience caused to all our passengers." I read the message again, yet again, disbelievingly. Did this really happen? I never knew of all flights getting cancelled simultaneously.

How could that be possible? And yet, here it was, the message from the airlines itself. Now what?

That message had yet again made a decision on my behalf. I was going to spend Master's Birthday and attend the *Bhandara* after all, till the 25th. Something happened at that moment and a sudden calmness came over me. As if a healing balm had been rubbed all over me and I was at peace. The war, anger, argument, vitriol all went away and a gentle smile took its place.

I showed the message to my daughter and we walked back to the tent. I did not attend any satsangh and I did not step out of the tent area either. Till we headed for the airport again, my daughter and I ended up having the best mom-daughter time. We volunteered in the kitchen, canteen, cleaning and wherever else we could make ourselves useful, we did together. I played with her and during satsangh time I sat by her side and did my *Puja*. True to her word, not once did she disturb me, she happily went about her play, reading or simply watched me meditate.

With everything working in my disfavour something favourable changed inside me that *Bhandara*. I finally knew I was home, my search had definitely ended. I was here, in Sahaj Marg, to stay. This was it, my destination, my goal, the answer to all my questions would be available here, and it was but a matter of time (the attitude to quit at the drop of the hat went). My wandering mind had finally found its resting spot. Yet again, I had no words to describe. What happened, what I had received, I still don't know. I was very incoherent when my prefect asked me about my first *Bhandara* experience. I had not met Master; much worse, I failed to attend even one Satsangh. Even then the ambrosial cloud seemed to have burst over my head and I felt cleansed, empty and brimming with immense possibility; many unspoken emotions for this amazing Path.

I packed our bags, and spent the rest of the day with my daughter, took her to the canteen, played with her inside the tent. I would bid adieu tomorrow and probably search for a new path, I did not know. Whatever fate had in store for me; peace reigned for the rest of the day and I did my experience. I had not met Master; much worse, I failed to attend even one Satsangh. Even then the ambrosial cloud seemed to have burst over my head and I felt cleansed, empty and brimming with unspoken emotions for this amazing path. My journey had just begun …

Learnings

In 2008-2009, Master visited North India often. Every visit had a transit halt in Delhi or Gurgaon, in the state of Haryana. My ever enthusiastic and fanatical prefect was always informed about these visits. Not only would she charge ahead and make plans to go to the airport to greet Master, or meet Him wherever he was halting, or accompany him with the convoy. She would pool resources, goad us into hiring a taxi and race to the place where Master was headed for. Anything and everything to be able to meet Him was fair and the end justified the means. That was the gist of the story.

As a new *Abhyasi* I never had the nerve to say no to her. That aside, I too would be greedy for a chance to be able to meet Master. This *Bhandara* I could not go and visiting Chennai was always a distant dream. So, when master travels half way across the country, it was simply too irresistible a chance to resist.

Apart for the many times I waited in the long queues to get a mere glimpse of Him, in Gurgaon ashram, I distinctly recall two incidents where I waited for hours and hours and returned home without meeting, yet with profound learning.

It was in the month of December, Master had come to Delhi and was to proceed for Gurgaon the following morning where He would conduct satsangh. We all received information that Master was tired, he would like to rest tonight and thus, abhyasis were requested not to crowd in front of the brother's place (where master was halting for the night). By the time we received this information we were already halfway to our destination and decided to override the instructions. With my recent discovery of my daughter's birthday and her being special (my imbecilic conclusion), I was certain I could ignore the announcement and Master would surely meet me, I had His Guru's birthday partner with me. Through the car drive my daughter kept asking me if master would meet her and would she get a chance to shake hands with him. I very confidently kept assuring her that, of course, master would meet her. She is 30th April born and her name is 'Bhargavi. It is funny how master has repeatedly shown me the mirror and pointed out my stupidities to me. It is like the peeling of an onion; layer by layer of such befuddled misunderstandings and illogical conclusions. Many *abhyasis* had left by the time we reached. We were also asked to leave, because Master would like to rest. He decidedly would not step out today. Again, we turned a deaf ear and set up camp on the brother's front porch.

It was December and very soon it was dark and cold. My daughter was getting fidgety with the long wait and I was getting tense with uncertainty. Would he not come out today? But I had Bhargavi with me, how could he not come out to meet her?

Another *Abhyasi* sister was crying by the door, begging to be allowed to go inside, she wanted to meet master, she was in grave pain and needed to see him. She sobbed her heart out and finally she was allowed to go inside and got her chance to meet master!

I began to wonder if I should have cried too. Seeing this, my daughter asked if Master did not wish to meet her? How come that lady went in and we were still waiting. And in came the final thundering order to leave the premises immediately. So, we huddled back into the car and through the drive back home I sat stupefied, wondering why Master did not want to meet Bhargavi! What had I done again? I had definitely erred somewhere, but where? My daughter cried her heart out blabbering, "Master will never meet me. I will die without meeting Master. You said he would meet me. I was special. I am not special. You lied to me. He will never meet me. I will die like this, without ever meeting Master!" I don't know where she got all that from, but it kept ringing in my ears for days to come.

The two lessons I learned were that dates and names were irrelevant. Second more important lesson, obey Him.

In less than a month Master visited Delhi again, a transit halt on his way to Jaipur, the state of Rajasthan. I was careful this time. I obeyed all the instructions. And despite my prefect insisting that we again gate crash the brother's place, I politely refused to comply. Instead I cajoled my husband and booked a taxi to Jaipur. I packed my girl again not because of her birthday date but I was hoping to be able to meet Master and she would be delighted. I was trying to do everything right and by the book. I was very hopeful of meeting Master. Jaipur ashram was just being inaugurated and was not very crowded. Master was in relatively better health and not rushed for time either. So, my prospects of meeting Master seemed bright.

It is funny, that when I did everything wrong I could not meet Him, and when I did everything right too, the result was disappointment again. The minute we entered the place where Master was put up we were told that Master went inside to rest. He would be leaving for another venue in an hour's time. If I wanted to meet Him I should head for that place immediately. I rushed my daughter back to the hotel, freshened her up, gave her something to eat and headed for the said venue. The minute we entered the hall Satsangh started, I had to wait outside. Then Master conducted a meeting for prefects so again, I continued to wait outside. By then, my daughter was convinced that we would be met with failure, yet again. But I was still hopeful. Master came out of the meeting and proceeded to return to the guesthouse. That was when my heart sank. I dared not break the queue and forge my way to the front. It was thanks to my friend and her unassuming love for Master, she dragged me and posted herself in front of Master and said, "Hello Master!"

Master gave a look of recognition and said, "Where are you?" Shalini replied, "I am presently residing in Noida Master. We shifted last year. This is Sharanya, a new *Abhyasi*."

I folded my hands and said, "Namastey Master."

He gave me a cursory glance, nodded His head and headed for the car. He was about to get inside when a young boy shouted, "Master! I am 16years old, but I want to join meditation today. Please give me sitting!"

Master stopped in tracks (I distinctively remember His joyous expression, and the way His eyes suddenly lit up) and called out, "Santosh! What are you searching for, and where are you!

This boy is right here. Look at him! Someone give him a sitting and get him started please!"

He blessed the boy and shook hands with him, said something exclusively to him and got into the car. That question he had asked my friend seemed to have been directed at me. And this too, this small exchange with the young boy, seemed to have played itself out for my sake. Shalini, my friend was in the mission for many years, already a prefect and into a lot of volunteer work. She had the comfort level to walk up to Him, look into His eyes and speak to Him. Where was I? With what nerve was I taking up His time? What special work had I done to be able to stand in front of him?

And that boy, at the tender age of 16 he was eager to start a life of spiritual and material balance. Master wanted every young person to lead a balanced successful life and not enter spirituality because of past failures and to get rid of some miseries and frustrations. That boy was a reminder of my wasted years, and that I did not have time to squander further. Where was I really? I had joined this Mission with a very selfish motive of personal progress and was still stuck with that goal. I neither had the magnanimity in me nor the understanding of that 16-year-old.

I did meet Master in Jaipur. But that question and the small interlude with that boy stayed with me for long. My urge to see Him or be in his presence when he visited Delhi did not reduce. Whenever he came to Delhi I attended satsangh. But I never had the nerve to walk up to Him after that Jaipur incident. My introspection and search for 'Real Goal' took a different turn.

Our prayer is: "O'Master! Thou art the real goal of human life. We are yet but slaves of wishes, putting bar to our advancement. Thou art the only God and power to bring us up to that stage."

Simple four lines with a world of depth and an all-encompassing, profound meaning. I am humbled time and again to be a part of this Mission. Where did they come from; these Masters? They are struggling every day, for worthless people like me, who are unable to come out of these mundane problems and daily squabbles. They are working tirelessly so that at least one amongst us can stand by their side and really 'see' them. Be bold enough to become one with them.

Attempts ...

Meeting master was still on my mind but before that I wanted to become a worthy *Abhyasi*. I wanted to be true to the method he had given us, follow the 10 maxims, and do volunteer work to be a part of the Mission as a whole. Keep running to Chennai or booking taxis and going to meet him where ever he went on his travels, all this stopped. For one, I did not feel that He may have approved, secondly, all these sudden, unplanned travels were taxing the family and lastly, I wanted to do what He has offered us properly; change myself so that I did not feel like cringing or disappearing into oblivion with the feeling of worthlessness when I stood in His presence. I never missed a single chance when he came to Delhi though. Settled with these thoughts I tried to follow all the three with due diligence, Method, Master and Mission.

I read Master's books and the uncountable anecdotes He had with His Master. And many *abhyasis* in my centre were *abhyasis* for long with many stories to narrate. Their interactions with Master were many, and every story sounded like music to my ears. It was as if He made every single person who came in touch with Him feel special, extraordinary and totally loved. Every incident was intoxicated with love for Him. I felt sad that I had joined so late, wasted so many years and now we were too many abhyasis in the Mission. The mission then was small and Master gave personal attention to almost every single Abhyasi. Now, Master had spread the mission worldwide and multi fold. It was impossible to meet all the abhyasis. Master was not in good health either. Meeting Him and demanding His personal time was unfair, unethical.

Mostly, I did contain my temptation and be content with listening to others' stories and attending Satsangh when Master visited Delhi. Every few months though, some frenzy overtook me and I made plans to visit Chennai. One such occasion was the New Year's Day of 2009. And the catalyst was this passage ...

"I used to wonder why this was necessary. After all, is it not enough that the Master comes to us? Whether you come to me or I come to you what difference does it make?

There is a small difference. He comes to us because of His divine love for us, we go to Him only when we start to love Him.

Now I would like to give you the example of candle. The candle goes wherever there is darkness and illuminates it. That is the Master going around and round to illuminate us, our hearts. But can the darkness ever come to the candle to be illuminated? That is what Master waits for when the Abhyasi come to Him. And that oracle can happen only between human beings, not between darkness and light. And it is possible only when love comes into the heart of the abhyasis, because then all idea of benefit, of growth, of getting something from the Master, they go. And love takes their place, then the Abhyasi thinks what he can do for the Master, what he can give to the Master." (Role of Master in Human Evolution: Parthsarthi Rajgopalachari --pg. 12)

30th December 2008, Chennai.

The Manapakkam ashram was decorated like a newlywed bride. But I don't recall much anymore. All I recollect is that

it was packed like sardines in a box. Abhyasis crawling like ants everywhere, unmindful of the crowd or sweat, they were enjoying, participating and adding to the air of festivity. I had not anticipated this crowd at all and was totally flummoxed. The dormitory was packed. We (I had again dragged the children) managed a small corner and quickly spread our foldable mattress to mark our territory. But by the time we could settle down another family came and crammed in too.

Master had just then retired for the day, but would be conducting a satsangh at 12:00 to herald the New Year on a prayerful note. The crowd was too much for me to handle and I could not bring myself to crowding in front of His cottage yet again. I felt like a vulture waiting to plunge on my unaware poor prey. Conclusively, I returned home without seeing my master.

I made a promise to myself that I would attend the *Bhandaras* henceforth and visit Chennai when Master invited us, as a group. This independent visit and crowding the ashram was taxing for Him, His health was already on the downside and we were adding to it with our long lines in front of His cottage begging, pleading and crying for His Darshan. I felt guilt laden and further depressed, and promised to refrain myself from repeating such feats.

Guru Poornima 2012 …

In His kindness, Master called our State (Uttar Pradesh) first for the following Guru Poornima and I was exultant. My being a disciplined *Abhyasi* paid off, He had called and thus I would surely get a chance to see Him. I could spend time with Him, listen to Him address us, with total impunity. The whole ashram came together and started preparing for Guru Poornima. We planned a ballet, spent excruciatingly long hours practicing, discussed endlessly about the ideal gift for Master and very soon the day to board the flight to Chennai arrived.

This time all was correct and I did not dream of not meeting Him, the thought of failure did not cross my mind. But fate always plans the most unexpected and surprises become shockers in a flash. We were invited for a week-long stay, from 2nd July to 8th July. My tickets were from 2nd to 5th. I was to leave on the 6th morning because my husband had an official tour, I had to get back to the kids.

We all arrived on 2nd July, and we were to perform the ballet the same evening. So, 2nd night we performed the ballet; Master saw it on the video from His cottage. He was unwell and had decided to stay in. After the ballet, He invited the participants inside the cottage. Unfortunately, the whole ashram got excited and became totally unruly. They jostled each other and behaved uncouth and maniacal. Master must have been disgusted, because in the middle of the chaos we were ordered to get back to our dormitories. The participants received a box of chocolates and Master refused to see anyone. He decided to call it a day.

I felt sick at the way we had behaved and fervently prayed that I would not be punished for our behaviour. Next day His health was a bit on the downside and He decided to stay in, again. 4th was Guru Poornima, and His health did not improve much. So, we wandered about in the ashram hoping He would be better the next day. Now, I was in a frenzy again. Three days gone. And this time I had done everything, every single thing by the book. I had very consciously behaved; controlled all my impulses at unruly and lunatic behaviour, in the hope that this time I would definitely be able to See Him. Now I had only one more day, the 5th of July. If He decided to stay in tomorrow as well, then I would be the worst jinxed person ever.

I have never cursed my fate so much as I cursed it that fated trip. Master was unwell on the 5th too. He did not come out. On the 6th morning I packed my suitcase and dragged my feet to the main gate. Head downcast I tried to avoid eye contact with everyone.

My prefect saw my face and trying to pacify me, said, "Why are you so sad? You are His favoured disciple. That's why He does not see the need to meet you, in person." She consoled me with give an analogy about the doctor seeing only the sick, and healthy patients don't need to be seen by the doctor.

Her kind remarks failed to soothe or embalm by broken heart. I continued to simmer and work myself up into an agitated angry woeful state. And I could neither contain my disappointment nor my tears. This was just not what I had anticipated. This was not what I thought I deserved either. I was angry at Him. He had no right to continuously reject someone who loved Him so earnestly; so truly and since so long. All the stuff I had read in the books about Him listening to the prayers of a craving heart were lies. Not a grain of truth in any of that. He seemed to favour every other person, except me. All the world was able to walk in, meet Him and be in His presence; deserving or not. Here, I always met with rejections or some introspective comment that left me pondering over my behaviour all the time. And to rub salt over my wounds He came out that on the 6th morning. He met all the *abhyasis,* sat amidst them and gave a heart-warming speech filled with humour and a very ruminative message. I was sitting at the airport crying over my rotten fate and He was amidst the *abhyasis* laughing and making them glow with love. Was I that undeserving? Maybe I was. Why did I repeatedly encounter failure and rejection? And yet with every such trip my determination to do more was reaffirmed. My love for Him grew and I pulled up my socks yet again to be worthy of Him. He would call me. I was still not doing things the way He wanted me to do. What was it that I was still missing?

And my march to inch my way closer to Him continued. I started volunteer work in all earnestness, wanting to serve, be of some use to Him, and contribute towards the growth of the Mission. And, I also attended my first training program in Kharagpur. That was another revelation to me as to how little I really knew about this wondrous Mission, this miraculous Method and our magnanimous Master.

Kharagpur Training Program:

This was my first training program and it came 3 years after joining this path. I am not sure if it is just me or most of us are structured the same way. I learn everything fast and forget too, with greater speed. That is why I face the same situation time and time again. My lessons never seem to get firmly embedded, and become second nature to me. I kept slipping often, face the inevitable consequences, and get back on track for a while and slip again.

My Kharagpur training was a revelation in many ways. I had this complacent 'know it all' feeling about Master, Method and Mission. In the last 3 years I had attended more than one congregation, was regular with my practice, and always attended my weekly Satsangh. Being a voracious reader most of the Mission books were also done and dusted. Nothing more could be learnt and this training program was going to be another feather to my already feathered cap.

Kharagpur is in West Bengal and apart from IIT Kharagpur, this place is a small township, laid back and with zero distractions of the modern world. Amidst this rural backdrop our ashram has resident prefects, who live there and volunteer in the upkeep, maintenance and running of the ashram. Full-fledged training programs are conducted regularly and abhyasis arrive in batches from all over India. They stay in the ashram premises where boarding and lodging is provided free of cost. Most of the prefects and trainers live in modest quarters and manage on meagre resources. They have no other avocation or entertainment here. The closest metro city with modern amenities, malls, cinema or any entertainment is Kolkata; which is a 5-hour drive away.

A few things struck me, one- these prefects came all the way from their home towns and volunteered here because Master had asked them to do so. They had taken voluntary retirement from their jobs and dedicated their life to service. I had a long way, very long road to travel still.

Secondly, the ashram itself is world class. It has the best collection of books ranging from fact, fiction, philosophy, history, science, medicine and the holy texts of all religions. Master was spending so much money on all this infrastructure. He was trying to nurture us to become introspective, encouraging us to read about other religions. He had the courage to put every other faith's scripture and philosophy within our reach. He wanted us to accept the mission through learning and self-experience. I have practiced other philosophies before joining this mission. But I have never experienced this anywhere. The first thing that I encountered was being subtly coerced to exclude all else, and many don'ts. Here it is the opposite. We are not threatened or manipulated to follow this path alone. We need not fear any sin or the wrath of the Guru if we decide to leave this path and join a different one. We are free to think and use our discerning ability, decide for ourselves. There is no Damocles sword hanging over my head this time. This freedom is rare and unique.

Another strange revelation was, with all the other paths I had tried before this, the Guru always seemed totally out of bounds, unreachable. I could never dream of standing next to the Guru, let alone attaining His heights of spiritual advancement. Here, the Guru was handing us everything on a platter. He gave me the hope of being able to become like Him, and maybe become Him too! He was with me every step of the way and constantly assuring me that this was possible. Enlightenment was within reach, and in this very lifetime. All I needed to do was be co- operative and willing. I had never known any path where the Master worked so hard to create Masters because He did not aspire for followers. Was this possible anywhere else? He was distributing himself (transmission is the life force of life), of His own free will for us and in return he was bearing the brunt of all the unwilling, stubborn and unyielding abhyasis, who were resisting His attempts to change us and bring forth the goodness in us.

Of our Ten Maxims, the first maxim states:

"Rise before dawn. Offer your prayer and puja (meditation) at a fixed hour preferably before sunrise, sitting in one and the same pose. Have a separate place and seat for worship. Purity of mind and body should be specially adhered to"

On this trip, I learnt that Master kept requesting us to retire for the day by 10:30pm. Waking up before dawn and finishing meditation before sunrise was for our individual benefit and speedy progress. And sleeping by 10:30pm was to enable Master to work on us while we slept. We resist in our conscious wakeful state; thus, He is forced to work on us when we are asleep. Such was our plight and yet He remained uncomplaining and ever magnanimous. If only I could comply with these Maxims, I would be half way there on the path of self- realization.

Poignant of all learnings came on the last day. We had a group activity in which we were all given instructions and asked to reach from point A to point B, blindfolded. The first time, we were given a guide, and the second time we were asked to accomplish the same journey on our own. Now, the instructions were easy and I already had a guide, for the first round. So, what if I was blindfolded, my eyes were right by my side to guide me. In the first-round I bumped into a chair, and the fellow participant, who was acting as my guide, gently steered me and instructed me to change course. I accomplished this trip successfully and was ready to do the second trip on my own.

I had made mental notes, landmarks and all I needed to do was follow them. I thought I was prepared, and hence did not need a guide anymore. But, even before the race could begin properly I started to fumble and crashed into bush. That fall flummoxed me and my direction, position and the mental notes I had made for myself, all flew out of the window. I stood there for a few seconds and tried to calm myself, so that I could reorient myself, make my way back and start again.

It wasn't about winning anymore; completing the journey was at stake now. I stood there trying to collect my thoughts when I heard my guide's voice gently whisper by my side, "You are going the wrong way, turn around and start walking straight".

That voice was like a Godsend! We were to do this journey on our own, yet the guide was aware of my stupidity and over confidence and was by my side, guiding me the whole time; much like our Master. He knows of our arrogance and stupidity and in His infinite love and wisdom, incessantly keeps His eyes on us. We are never out His sight. I was ashamed of myself. A simple game, the simplest of instructions and I had erred so badly. I shamefacedly continued my walk and covered the distance. When I removed the blindfold, I was confronted with yet another blunder I had made. I was the only one standing at this spot. The other participants were already at their destination and that was somewhere else! They were all looking at me and I looked back at them, with my guide right behind me, wearing a weak smile. I asked my guide where I had blundered, and she explained that I had started on the same track, fallen and changed course. She had whispered the right direction and yet I had derailed again and ended at this wrong spot. I did not hit any road blocks and was not stumbling either so she simply followed me, on the wrong path! I would eventually remove the blindfold and realize my folly. In my own stupidity, I did not hear the instructions correctly. What was worse was that I simply assumed that both the trips were from the same Point A to same point B, and how mistaken was I.

I am a Behavioral counselor and Psychotherapist by profession and my key skill is 'listening'. Listening with interest, listening with empathy and listening correctly; these should be my core skills. This simple game had proved me wrong on all counts. I was so self -absorbed, I think I was half deaf. I heard but did not listen to the instructions and neither was I humble enough to take the guidance offered the second time, and reach the right place! Even at that point I immediately set off on my own and reached the wrong spot. How many such mistakes I was making in my skill is 'listening'. Listening with interest, listening with empathy and listening correctly; these should be my core skills. This simple game had proved me wrong on all counts. I was so self -absorbed, I think I was half deaf. I heard but did not listen to the instructions and neither was I humble enough to take the guidance offered the second time and reach the right place! Even at that point I immediately set off on my own and reached the wrong spot. How many such mistakes I was making in my day to day events and decision-making process, I do not know. And how many times was my poor Master was coming to my rescue, trying to veer me and redirect me, I do not know that either. And to top it all, how many times was I, the blithering idiot that I am, not paying heed to Him and He had to face failure or defeat because of me, well I do not dare to know!

In retrospect, I feel that Kharagpur training put me on the lowest rung again. I was a beginner still and there was nothing I knew about this Method, Mission and least about my Master. How could I even begin to understand this person who worked tirelessly for no personal benefit, against so many odds, facing the possibility of failure and yet remained steadfast in His work, continued to shower me with love and never rebuked me.

I had a long, long way to go still. My desire to be of some use to the Mission could only be accomplished if I could become worthy enough to be of some service to Him and contribute to His work. I had to work on myself first, follow the method, path better, and live this path. Just following this path may take me some distance, but I wanted to walk the whole nine yards, become Him. For that I had to live this path. Following would make a follower at best, I wanted to be of some use to Him. Live with the pain and defeat He lives every day and yet continue to smile and shower love.

Learning-Changing ...

Metamorphosis may be a very small term to describe the possibility of change in oneself with diligent practice of this method. The change was ever so gentle and subtle that it caught me unawares and came to light very gradually. And the change I think, or rather, I have experienced, happens from the inside out. I continue to look the same, the persona did not change but I was going through a turn around on the inside. This tug of war of balancing my inside and outside also caused a lot of upheaval and the subtle changes could come to light only after a few years.

I joined Sahaj Marg with heavy baggage and most of me needed to be changed. I daresay that I was so full of self-disgust that it gave birth to an ardent desire for change. I was unhappy with everything; the way my life was getting wasted, and that everyone else seemed unreasonably happier than I was. I felt as if everything was rigged against me or was happening to deliberately goad me, and everyone was intent on criticising my good nature and find fault with me.

My co-relating 'change' as being synonymous with 'miracle' may have been the reason. I never noticed any change in myself, change could not be qualified as a miracle. Secondly, in Sahaj Marg, we do not encourage nor endorse this belief in miracles and we are seriously advised not to look out for or seek miracles. The first year flew juggling these mixed emotions and trying to get rid of such subconsciously adapted, unfruitful practices. Overcoming these ingrained habits and bringing a change in my lifestyle can probably be called my first miracle. Giving up temple worship was a miracle for me, but a most natural progression for a sincere abhyasi. Not worth being called a miracle. So how was I to show my change or how could I advocate myself?

If I arm twisted my family members, forced anyone, someone, to voice any change in me, the oft repeated non-committal could be summarized as, "You still want me to notice change; should you not be more self-aware now? Stop searching for things on the outside and ask yourself." Such comments would pierce me right through like a sharp dagger, and my journey inwards began.

This brought me to my next question; how had I changed really? My external appearance was the same as before, so what had changed? Much to my amazement the first response came from my husband himself; I overheard him one day saying, "The amazing change in my wife since she has joined Sahaj Marg is miraculous to me! It is as if Sahaj Marg has waved a magic wand over her; she is a very new, different person!"

So, there it was, Sahaj Marg had performed a miracle on me! The stubborn, negative me had changed to become a better person and was improving every day, truly a miracle!

A prefect, explaining the system to new abhyasis said, "Sahaj Marg is not about getting or gaining something. It is about changing and becoming someone!" The possibility of another miracle! A changed human being because of Sahaj Marg. Which path gives this reassurance and invites this self-enquiry? Which Guru reposes so much confidence in another human being of no caliber and encourages him/her to become divinized? Which system never says 'no' to anything and yet manages to help the aspirant in saying "no" or letting go of everything that is unnecessary. The transition was so smooth that I never realized I was letting go of anything! This mission had enabled the impossible. This mission allowed me, the stubborn egotistic me to change and chiselled away at the jagged, chaffed ends and set me on the road to becoming a better human being. Subtle changes happen every day and I realize them over a period of time. A small change that recently came to light was my thinking or reaction towards non-abhyasis or people continuing temple worship. I myself started off as a big devout and took a year to let go of my rigidity. This made me very happy and, on the flipside, may be egotistical too. I had developed an aversion of sorts towards temple goers, or idol worshippers. I was above that, and they were foolish, I was the wise one. I wanted to shake them up and make them realize how foolish they were or how futile what they were doing could be. Stepping inside a temple became a bit difficult and 'below my dignity'. Even in learning, 'good' ego raises its ugly head and I was actually 'not progressing'. All this is so subtle at a subconscious level that the realization happens without any noise. Out of the blue, during mediation, I realized my folly. Who was I to sit on judgment? And how was I any better than them? In fact, I was maybe worse, because I was into meditation and yet not really becoming the person I should become. I was still entangled with this superior- inferior idiocy and looking at others rather than focusing on improving myself. Now, I visit temples with equal reverence and humility, not for me, but because that is what is demanded of me. My prayer has changed from 'change them' to 'help them find their path of self–realization'. I started with self-loathe and gradually moved to self –love. Now I am trying to love all and try and hurt none. If this is not miraculous, then what else is?

All this system really demanded was my willingness. And I was more than willing to change. Thus, I was in a race against myself, competing with myself and setting expectations also, of myself. I still have lots in me that can be changed, but a lot has changed too. I am less angry, more cheerful, and more competitive with myself, less in competition with the world. I have no time to hold onto grudges or brood over other's wrongs. I am busy peeling my own layers and discovering myself anew every day. Moreover, I know I have my miracle within me, I will change. Sahaj Marg, me in Sahaj Marg - both are miracles and I aspire to realize another miracle, namely; living up to my Master's expectations and becoming what He has envisioned for me.

At His Feet

Kharagpur training was another turning point for me. I no longer wanted to be an *abhyasi* following this path. My goal changed from that day onwards. I wanted to breathe and live this path, serve Him to the best of my ability, that was the only possible way to repay Him. Of what use was I if I did my abhyas and nothing different happened in His life? He was risking everything to see at least one person emulate Him and stand by His side. It seemed to be my basic moral duty to be able to make Him proud. My craving to stand in front of Him, at His feet became a burning desire.

I count myself as the most fortunate and unfortunate *abhyasi* of this mission. Five years down the line and I was still waiting to 'meet' Him. I had made umpteen attempts and failed umpteen times, and I would continue to make those attempts and wait for Lady luck to smile on me. It was my misfortune and I had to work through it, accept and turn the events into my fortune.

What did I know of His ways? My ignorance was proven time and again and applying my brains needlessly was futile. This 'not being able to meet' Him was indeed my good fortune. This was what egged me on, pushed me to learn more, do more, and unleash my full potential. For such a lazy, laid back person, if I had met Master in the first attempt, maybe my *abhyas* would have also come to a grinding halt. I don't know, maybe my pig-headed self would have decided that I was realized already, had He met me in the first attempt, blessed me, and the children, what else did I need? I don't think I can fathom His ways nor do I have the intelligence to do so.

From the vitriolic and embittered person I used to be, I had definitely come a long way. Back in 2008, the whole world was conspiring to ensnare me into some abysmal hole and bury me in it. Today, without meeting Him, He has somehow weaved His magic. I won't say I have arrived, but I can definitely say, I am on the way, and learning and improving every day.

Finally, sometime in March 2013, I was called to Chennai, where Master resided; and asked to commence my prefect's training (trainer who can impart the steps of this method to other seekers). The last sitting is giving by Master, and he gives the abhyasi the prefect's certificate, authorizing the person to commence work. It was thus confirmed, I would be in His presence and I definitely knew I was on the verge of realizing my five-year dream.

My friend suggested gifts that I could take for Master, things He appreciated. I weighed all options given; Master is fond of classical music and plays the flute, He loves coffee (partial to Persian Coffee), Murukku and Mysore pak. He is an avid reader and a connoisseur of almost everything! I could have bought, any one of the above; all of the above, I was spoilt for choice. Yet, I could not make up my mind. Some said, "Take pictures of your family members so you can show them to Master when you speak to Him". I asked my husband to take a few pictures of the three of them together and mail them to me. One part was accomplished, but until the last day my ideal gift eluded me. What can one buy for someone who wanted nothing for Himself? What could I possibly gift Him, which was not already His? Even if a sliver of Him reflected in me, that alone was a worthy gift for Him. All else seemed inadequate and worthless.

That I could live up to His expectations, was all I could pray for as a gift. In fact, not even a gift, it was a miniscule token of the immense gratitude I felt.

The momentous dawn finally came, and in a few hours' time I would be face to face with my Master. I had been waiting for this chance for a long time; to be in His august presence. I had bought a saree to celebrate or mark this defining occasion and felt rather silly that I was worried if it was beautiful enough to be worn in His presence. I was a bag of mixed emotions. How the mind could conjure so many conflicting and such varied thoughts and emotions, I still wonder! Everything was racing through my mind with crystal clarity and everything went blank in the next moment. To add to my flurry, I was informed that I would be doing the last part of the journey with our Master- to - be, Brother Kamlesh. This made me happy and a bit more flustered. I was going to meet the New Master already, my luck had not just turned, it was more like a windfall!

The drive to Master's residence seemed very long, with Kamlesh Master sitting in the front, beside the chauffeur, and me in the backseat; I was trying not to hear my thudding heart, praying Kamlesh Bhai could not hear it either. Kamlesh Brother asked me my name and I answered, "Sharanya" and went silent. We continued the journey in silence. He was chatting with the other brother who was driving us and seemed to be in a jovial mood. In contrast, I was in the backseat; outwardly calm and a raging storm within; tight lipped and like a zombie; mentally replaying the trivial things I wanted to ask Him, tell Him.

At last, we reached Gayatri, Master's house. The house is so calm, yet so vibrant and alive, noiselessly telling me so many things and soothing my frayed nerves. Everyone in the house was up and about doing their own work. It was 6:00 am and this house looked like it had never slept at all. The aroma of fresh coffee mixed with the fragrance of fresh jasmine flowers filled the house. I waited to be called inside and fervently kept praying to stay calm. I was not tense, I was not relaxed either. I was oscillating between the two, waiting to meet Him.

In no time I was before Him, the one person I aspired to meet since I raced behind his Golf cart. He was right in front me, asking me my name! It took all my strength and willpower not to break down, fall at His feet and embrace Him tightly; never to let go … it was sheer joy, gratitude, awe, love and I barely managed to whisper my name. He said it aloud three times as if He was trying to help me fathom the true purport of my name. My name itself means 'surrender' and all I had to do was live by my name; surrender to Him. I had no other aspiration either. My name sounded most unique and special coming from Him. I asked nothing, said nothing; after the sitting, I bent, touched his feet, took His blessings and left the room with a heart filled with His love, crying all the way back, His voice echoing in my ears and His gaze following me. Ever since, I am never alone. I could have asked something, said something or at least taken a photo with Him. Everyone who meets Him has some keepsake to show off, and here I was returning empty handed. After a five year long wait, I did not have any token with me to take back home and show my family; nothing, yet again, to talk about.

I met Him after five long years in the Mission and went in empty handed, teary eyed and with a heart throbbing so fast I thought it would burst open any second. And I had returned with a feeling of having received everything and more than I could possibly imagine.

It is rather funny the way my beloved Guru taught me my life lessons and made the egotistic me experience, realize and understand His presence and role in my life. Just the message I needed, at the right time; nothing more and nothing less. This path simply grows in you and helps you grow from within, probing, yet gently nurturing and revealing the right thing at the right time. He saved me from myself.

The Journey Continues ...

I met Him but once. That is all. My luck ran dry after that. He was too ill to grace us with His presence at the Bhandaras and duties at home kept me grounded in Delhi. I could not visit

Chennai nor attend a Bhandara for the next year and a half. And for someone who had planned to ask, tell and share so many things with Him, when I finally did meet Him, I went blank and tongue tied. All my conscious thought was in conflict, divided between exercising restraint as I was on the verge of breaking down whilst the other half was focused on trying to unabashedly soak Him up, bathe in the radiance and light His presence transmitted. I feel humbled to be a part of this Mission. Needless to say, I once again had very little to narrate back home. And yet again, I left Chennai with a heavy heart, crying all the way back home. I did not want to go home. I would have given anything to continue to be there, at His feet, be of service. He taught me what love really meant, to love without expectations, to be able to love one and all, however challenging it may be. He taught me to oversee the faults of others by gently showing me the mirror every time and helping me correct myself first. He taught me to be emotionally free, being unburdened and fly away mentally. Physically, I am still bound by duties and responsibilities but emotionally I soar the skies, free and ecstatic. He taught me to say the right thing and move on, do the right thing and stay firm, accept and surrender to unsavoury happenings and not hold grudges. All the credit goes to Him and this wondrous path I am trying to live by.

I have ceased to be my old self after that. The person that left home looks and behaves the same, but my heart belongs to Him and strives to do something, anything, in His name, His service. Nothing matches the depth of what I feel for Him or equates with what He has done for me. So, I cannot repay this debt ever, but I feel humbled and honoured just to be able to walk this path and emulate Him, give Him a reason to be proud of me.

I think I am doubly blessed, even though I had to wait five years to stand before Him, I was blessed by Him and His successor in the same meeting. Else I am sure I would never have been able to meet Kamlesh Master. Master handed over the reins to Kamlesh Master and left us on the 20th of December 2015. But as they say, "To live in the hearts you leave behind is immortality."

He lives on; in fact, He is ... therefore ... I am ...

Acknowledgements:

Apart from being extraordinarily fortunate to have so many mentors in my life, I am surrounded by many friends, brothers and sisters who have showered me with love and more love. Our ashram and my neighbourhood are verily the most propitious places; nurturing love and family bonding. We all were a huge family, we still are. Today, I am so many miles away, yet we are in touch regularly. We are aware of each other's problems and try to help as much as we can. There is no feeling of malice or competition amongst us. This group is honest with both, criticism and praise. They have taught me to love, love without expectation, and love freely in abundance and feel loved always. Distances have become irrelevant; we always are together, with each other. This group has helped me practice, emulate Master's quote: Love all whom He loves …

Thank you, all of you. You have changed me in more ways than I can explain or elucidate. I am not writing any names for the fear of excluding a single one and hurting any one of you. I love you all and I am very humbled to be a part of your life.

Special thank you to Kalpana Saxena, the sketches (in this journal) of our ashrams are her effort. Thank you Kalpana, for doing this for me; taking time out of your busy schedule and helping me out.

And last but not the least, a heartfelt thank you to my sister, Rajni and her partner David. Amidst their hectic and busy schedule, they took time out for me. They patiently edited chapter by chapter, put in the images in the right place and breathed life into this journal. Thank you, sis and thank you, David. This would have never seen daylight if you both had not helped me.

Lightning Source UK Ltd.
Milton Keynes UK
UKHW051153270219
338089UK00004B/56/P